THE MAN IN THE MIRROR

J. DARRELL TURNER

© 2023 J. Darrell Turner

All Rights Reserved.

Unless otherwise noted, all scripture quotations are taken from the King James Version.

Cover by Bridgett Henson Ministries

Published by:
Empowered Publications
66 Academy Lane
McIntosh, Alabama 36553

ISBN 978-1-943033-86-7

DEDICATION

WHEN I was a young evangelist in the 1980s, I was given some sermons by a Texas Pastor by the name of B.H. Clendennen. After I listened to a few of those messages, I was never the same. I began to call him and have long conversations on the phone, with questions concerning the "flesh and spirit", and also about "sanctification". He graciously and scripturally answered them all. He always had time for a young preacher and his many questions.

In the latter part of 1991, we became friends and then I considered him my mentor until his death in 2009. His impact on a generation of ministers and believers will only be fully known in eternity. At his side was his faithful wife Janice Clendennen. She was an inspiration to all who met her. Since Brother Clendennen's home going, Sister Clendennen has been a source of encouragement and strength to me.

I could never repay what they both have so graciously poured into my life and ministry.

I therefore dedicate this book to the Memory of B.H. Clendennen and in Honor of Janice Clendennen.

Your reward is sure.

J. Darrell Turner

CONTENTS

1. Sanctified, Now What? 5

2. The Man In The Mirror 9

3. The Man In The Mirror And The Merry-Go-Round 13

4. Searching For The Answer 19

5. What Then Can Change Me? 23

6. The Second Mirror 29

Chapter 1

Sanctified, So Now What?

HAVING been in and around what some have termed "traditional Pentecost" most of my life, I have been very familiar with the doctrine of sanctification. The particular Pentecostal movement I was brought up in taught what was called the "second definite work" or "instantaneous" message of sanctification; that somewhere between the experience of salvation and being baptized in the Holy Ghost, one would be wholly sanctified. After my call to preach the Gospel and during my early years of study and preparation, I came to understand that there were other scriptural views and teaching concerning sanctification. Some movements taught "progressive" sanctification, where the believer experiences the "ongoing" work of sanctification throughout their Christian lives.

In the early days of Pentecost, each was adamant that their particular view was correct.

Early on I struggled with the teaching that we were once and for all instantly sanctified, and in that experience, it rendered the "old nature" or the "old man" forever dead and crucified. What seemed implied in most of the teaching and preaching I heard early on was that your fleshly struggles as a new believer were mainly due to not yet having experienced sanctification. I found that after I had truly been born again, prayed for sanctification, and baptized in the Holy Ghost, I still at times found myself in a battle with my flesh! Even though I considered the old man dead, he would periodically try to resurrect! I could not understand as a young believer how this could be. Was I sanctified or not? I knew beyond a shadow of a doubt that I had been born again, that I had been baptized in the Holy Ghost with the initial evidence of speaking in other tongues as the Spirit gave utterance, yet the warfare continued. There were those then that said, "Your problem is that sanctification is progressive and so *this* is your answer." So, I scripturally considered this view as well. Actually, I found the Bible teaches that sanctification is instantaneous and progressive, or the word I commonly use, "continuous", and the Bible teaches many types and experiences of sanctification.

I have not set out to write another book on the doctrine of sanctification. Many great theologians have written extensive works on the subject, but what is amazing to me, is that most seem not to totally agree on their teaching, even if they are a part of the same denomination or movement. I once read that John Wesley in his understanding of the doctrine of sanctification stated that, he believed what many term "entire sanctification" in which the believer could become so sanctified that they would not even be tempted by sin! Yet he stated that he had not reached such a state of "entire sanctification," nor did he believe the Apostle Paul had ever attained to such an experience! Dear friends if it has been determined that neither Brother Paul nor Brother Wesley ever reached such a sanctified state, need I say more? I am convinced that we can say with great confidence that the scripture teaches the work or works of sanctification from the new birth to the glorious moment we are changed from these vile bodies.

My only purpose in my brief discussion concerning sanctification is that no matter how sanctified we are or become, no matter how oft we experience the various and wonderful types of it, we are still at times in the Christian life going to battle this flesh. *"For the flesh lusteth against the Spirit, and the Spirit against the flesh: and these are contrary the one to the other: so that ye cannot do the things that ye would" – (Gal. 5:17).*

Lusteth in the Greek is epithumeō – ep-ee-thoo-meh'-o. It means to set the heart upon, that is, long for (rightfully or otherwise): - covet, desire, would fain, lust (after).

I know some will immediately become argumentive and begin to state that because we are "crucified with Christ", "dead to the old nature of sin", and "that old things have passed away" and "all things have become new", that we should never have any more issues with the flesh! I am aware and in total agreement with all these wonderful scriptures that speak of the "changed and newness of life" of the believer. I can assure you that I am walking 180 degrees from the life I experienced before being born again. Let me respectfully state that with true thankfulness, before I venture down the road to what I am convinced God gave me some years ago, to help me and all believers to be victorious over this flesh, this "Man In The Mirror" syndrome!

While I've had the privilege of knowing some of the greatest Christians in the world, some of whom were Pastors, Evangelist, Missionaries, etc. I have prayed with, preached with and fellowshipped with some of the Godliest men and women of our time, spread out over the Pentecostal vine. I've never met one, not even a single one of these precious, Godly, devout and praying saints who did not battle with some fault of that flesh! Not one, who didn't at some time or the other struggle with again what I will call throughout this book the "Man In The Mirror" syndrome in their Christian life. Are you shocked? Would you think that I'm just being critical and judgmental? These precious saints were the "jewels" of the Master in my eyes and heart. Many of them are the ones I would turn to for prayer and instruction because of my upmost confidence in their walk with Christ, yet they would "all" tell you that somewhere in the journey to the Celestial City they had "struggles," and they had "faults," that their flesh would battle against the Spirit and the Spirit against the flesh. For those trying to pretend otherwise it is just that, "pretending." God doesn't think to highly of "pretenders." He regards those who are honest with Him and themselves, and those of a pure heart, who want to have victory over sin and the flesh. Let me state emphatically, that I'm not referring to an individual who is walking in a lifestyle of sin and transgression! According to the Apostle James that person is not even born again. I am, and will, throughout the book refer to the one who has a heart to be like Christ in every way, who desires to be perfect and holy!

If you see yourself as "perfect" and "faultless," the one who doesn't have any struggles with the flesh and the Spirit, then you will likely want to end your journey with me now. But those who want to know the blessed and glorious truth of how to have victory over the "Man In The Mirror," then prayerfully lets continue on.

Chapter 2

The Man In The Mirror

AFTER many years in the Christian faith and preaching ministry, I finally came to the conclusion that, way too many preachers in the past have failed the sheep, in at least two vital areas: Teaching and example! In fact, I personally believe my journey and growth in the Christian life as a young man could have been advanced in understanding the battle between flesh and Spirit. If someone would have been willing to admit, that yes, men and women of God who are anointed, holy and used in ministry, sometimes have struggles and battles with the flesh, that we don't always win so well!, that would have greatly benefited my life. Much of the past preaching usually alluded that the preacher was the "pillar of perfection" and to not measure up cast doubt on your salvation and love for a Holy God! I know to some this sounds harsh, unfair, and judgmental. I put myself in this category, because that's the way I learned ministry – by example – and it took a lot of years for me to understand that it's one thing to preach about failure and battles with the flesh, but the greatest preaching brings us into the revelation of the truth, that I can overcome, I can be victorious and live a life of victory over the works of the flesh and sin!

This book was born from a sermon that the Lord had given me in answer to a lot of prayer; actually years of prayer! In preaching Camp Meetings, Conventions, and Ministry Conferences around the nation and the world, I often mentioned a verse that I sensed deep in my spirit was at least part of the answer I was searching for. After some time, the Lord gave me the second part of what would bring me to a better understanding of the Christian struggle with this flesh. Because I had not been correctly taught as a young Christian concerning the battle of flesh and spirit, it was only after some years of ministry that one of the greatest Pentecostal preachers of our generation became a mentor to me and helped me to understand that, as long as we were in this world there would always be an attempted resurrection of the "old man" or "old nature" in the life of the believer. He helped me to comprehend what someone should have been willing and vulnerable enough to admit, that if he, "the old nature" raised his ugly head in our lives, we were not to "throw in the towel" and become listed among the backslidden and spiritually shipwrecked, but we were to make an altar and submit ourselves unto God, resist the devil, and he would flee from us! This man of God helped me to understand that, just because I had been sanctified instantly by the blood of Christ and was continuously being sanctified by the word and Holy Spirit, it did not exempt me from battles with the "old nature." My old mentor is in heaven now, but as long as I live, I will owe him a debt of Christian gratitude for helping me to break free of the teaching that: once sanctified, the battle is over. This helped me to understand what God revealed to me many years later concerning the "Man In The Mirror" syndrome.

The scripture I read, quoted, and struggled with is found in James 1:22-24. *"But be ye doers of the word, and not hearers only, deceiving your own selves. For if any be a hearer of the word, and not a doer, he is like unto a man beholding his natural face in a glass: For he beholdeth himself, and goeth his way, and straightway forgetteth what manner of man he was."*

When I say that I struggled, I simply mean I found myself in this verse. I realized that most of my Christian life I battled what I later phrased the "Man In The Mirror" syndrome. With this verse as my text I would lead into the message I am convinced the Lord gave me. Often, "seasoned" pastors and ministers shared with me how it impacted their lives!

In such times when there is such a powerful verse that God

is using to teach me a very important or life changing truth, I find myself going to some of the old Bible commentators of the distant past, those whose wonderful insight on the scriptures I've come to appreciate.

One is Adam Clarke, whose poetic words bring a clearer meaning to James 1:22-24. Let us read it, "Beholding his natural face in a glass – This metaphor is very simple, but very expressive. A man wishes to see his own face, and how, in its natural state, it appears; for this purpose, he looks into a mirror, by which his real face, with all its blemishes and imperfections, is exhibited. He is affected with his own appearance; he sees deformities that might be remedied; spots, superfluities, and impurities, that might be removed. While he continues to look into the mirror he is affected, and wishes himself different to what he appears, and forms purposes of doing what he can to render his countenance agreeable. On going away, he soon forgets what manner of person he was, because the mirror is now removed, and his face is no longer reflected to himself; and he no longer recollects how disagreeable he appeared, and his own resolutions of improving his countenance. The doctrines of God, faithfully preached, are such a mirror; he who hears cannot help discovering his own character, and being affected with his own deformity; he sorrows, and purposes amendment; but when the preaching is over, the mirror is removed, and not being careful to examine the records of his salvation, the perfect law of liberty, James 1:25, or not continuing to look therein, he soon forgets what manner of man he was; or, reposing some unscriptural trust in God's mercy, he reasons himself out of the necessity of repentance and amendment of life, and thus deceives his soul."

Now we have the scriptural basis for "The Man In The Mirror"! Who is he? He is all of us!

Chapter 3

The Man In The Mirror And The Merry-Go-Round

IT is without a doubt that one, if not the greatest battles of our hearts, is the continual fulfillment of these verses in relation to our own personal walk with God. In the pages of this book, you will find that I am going to be open, personal and vulnerable in dealing with this from my own journey. I am not living in an illusion. I've been a Christian and minister for several decades. All honest believers will see yourself here!

How often since I started on this journey of the Christian life have I come face-to-face with the "Man In The Mirror"? Having seen his faults, blemishes, defects and sins, seeing them often through what James calls the "mirror" of the word of God. The mirror was often before me to reveal. Every time I would set in a local Church setting, in a Camp Meeting or a Conference and hear a man or woman of God preach the word those defects and blemishes would be revealed. When I would be driving down the road and listening to a message on a CD, faults were illuminated. While in a conversation with some saint of God that was sharing with me the scriptures, or while reading the Bible, those superfluities would be brought to light as I saw myself in the mirror of God's holy word!

After having seen them through the "mirror" of the word of God and revelation of the Holy Spirit, I would be greatly convicted at times, and often with a heavy sense of grief because of what I had seen in myself through the "holy mirror!" I can say that always – without exception – I would confess to the defects, the blemishes and God forbid, the sin of the creature I beheld in the "mirror" of God's holy word. I immediately begin with plans to make amends, to change, to do better! I knew that to please the Lord I must forsake the source of what was so adversely affecting the image I beheld. It was not someone else's image, but mine! Not the blemishes and defects of my brother sitting next to me on the pew, or my sister who had been singing in the choir, but mine!

The one thing with all of us is that when we are tempted, so often we somehow transpose someone else's faults over ours when the pain and conviction comes from the revelation. We begin to think about others who have more blemishes, other ministers who have greater defects and try to cloud the image of our hearts we've been given. Like someone who is looking at a disturbing x-ray of their heart and then reaches in the file to pull out someone else's image and place it on the screen over theirs. It might make us feel better, but it doesn't change the diagnosis, or the issue of our heart's condition.

I feel that I can honestly say, (though only God knows our hearts) I have always tried to be sensitive to what the Holy Spirit is revealing to me about my own heart. If He reveals, I'm guilty. I try to never blame anyone, or anything but myself when it comes to my own failures, faults or sins. I am not referring to situations, events etc. where I have certainly blamed someone else for the issues or results at hand. The wrongs and yes, the sins of the heart, only I am to blame. The casting of blame upon others cost Saul the kingdom and ultimately his soul.

After having seen myself in the "mirror" of God's word, I would always leave the setting where this "crisis" of the heart had transpired with made up mind, purpose of heart, and grand intentions. But then…

"For I know that in me (that is, in my flesh,) dwelleth no good thing: for to will is present with me; but how to perform that which is good I find not" – (Rom. 7:18).

As James 1:22-24 states, that after beholding our self in the mirror, we will walk away and find ourselves forgetting what we saw. As the minutes, hours and days would pass, I found the image and the memory of what I had witnessed in the holy mirror began to fade. Sadly, it almost always does.

Some years ago I was preaching in an annual Camp Meeting in Florida. I was sharing the pulpit with a fellow evangelist, alternating services. After the other evangelist had preached a "heart searching" message, a friend who was visiting the meetings sincerely said to me, "That sermon really stirred me. When I get home, I am going to make some changes, I am going to deal with these things the minister preached about." My reply to him was not with any sarcasm whatsoever, I was merely making a truthful statement, a lesson learned, and just confirming what James had written. I said to him, "Don't worry about it, in a few days it will all be gone. You'll forget about it." He gave me one of those looks, but I knew sadly what I was saying was true, almost without exception. How many times have believers gone to Sunday morning services and heard the preaching of the word of God, became convicted, saw their blemishes and sins in the holy mirror of God's word, and purposed in their hearts to deal with it, to change, only to leave that setting, and at times the altar, and after a few days had forgotten what they saw; and too often what they had promised to God concerning dealing with it.

Oh, the guilt, as I beheld the spots and blemishes in the mirror of His word. I would immediately confess and ask forgiveness for what I saw there. How dare I not acknowledge what God was revealing to me about "self!" I repeat, I have always tried to be sensitive to the revelation of my heart, to never try to make excuses, to just honestly cry out to Him, guilty!

What would I see there? The hardness of my heart, jealousy, envy, strife, covetousness, materialism, bitterness, malice, some hidden lust, need I say more? Over several decades of Christian life, the Holy Spirit has found and revealed things in my heart that I most often did not know was there, and to be honest, at the moment of revelation, the stinging, painful reality of what I saw was at times overwhelming! In me, I would think, how could this have been there, and I not be aware of it? How could it be that some hidden things are only revealed when the mirror of His holy word shines the light deep in the crevices and "marshy" places of our hearts? There have been times when the revelation came during prayer and fasting, reading a book, in a conversation with a godly brother or sister. It would be revealed in a moment and I could feel the "prick" in my heart of the Holy Spirit as conviction would open up the door to where this blemish and fault had been lying; at times dormant, but still there.

You have been there too, haven't you? Of course, I am not alone, though this brings me little comfort! Every single Christian has battled the "Man In The Mirror" syndrome! We've all ridden the "merry-go-round"! The uncountable times of confessing, repenting, promising to make amends, to forsake the blemishes and the faults we've seen! How many times have we "prayed-off the guilt" and then the memory of the revelation would fade, and then God by His mercy would again bring us before the "holy mirror," and there we would see and behold all the same defects and our lack, our need of more of the holiness of God and the whole agonizing process would be repeated!

How often have we sincerely declared from our hearts, Lord I'm going to deal with this blemish, I'm going to do more for your kingdom. I am going to pray more, fast more, study more, witness more, and get the victory over these issues of my flesh! How often have we beaten ourselves up over our failures? In my Christian journey progress has been made, there has been change in me, but at times I feel it was way too little and much too slow. Too often with these blemishes and defects, what should have taken days or weeks, or at the most months to see progress, has often taken years. I repeat again, I know I am not alone and as I've stated, that brings me little comfort. But dear reader, you know what I've stated is true! We've all ridden the "merry-go-round," we've all battled the "Man In The Mirror" syndrome!

Chapter 4

Searching For The Answer

IS there hope? With God and His son Jesus Christ there is always hope! He never intended for us to live on the perpetual "merry-go-round" or to struggle with the "Man In The Mirror" syndrome.

I know there are those who have attained a place in God where they have been changed from "glory to glory" and have experienced the life of victory, being transformed into His image! I have read about them in the Bible and in the books of Christian history. Certainly, they often beheld themselves in the "holy mirror." They saw the blemishes, faults and defects revealed there. They knew all about the "merry-go-round," yet somewhere in their Christian journey they found the answer. Oh God of heaven, how I longed for the answer! I was certain that since it was so important, and seemed so elusive, that it had to be complicated and mysterious. Yet I had read the answer countless times in my Bible reading, but my eyes seemed to have a veil over them. It is something I knew, but somehow was not grasping.

I've shared in preaching concerning this case in point, concerning "veils" from my childhood. I was raised up in the rural south. Born in 1959 I spent my adolescent years growing up in the Cumberland Mountains of Tennessee. When I was a boy, whenever someone in the community died, the corpse would be brought from the funeral home in the valley to the mountain and placed in the home of the family. Since no one had air conditioning, if it was summer, the windows of the home were opened, thus creating a problem with the flies coming into the house and lighting upon the corpse in the casket. To help with this issue, a thin veil was placed over the open casket to keep the flies off the corpse. This veil while serving a purpose also kept the viewers from seeing the loved one's corpse as clearly. These truths have been right before us in the word of God, but it seemed a veil was keeping me from seeing clearly what God intended.

I want to challenge our thinking and religious mindset here. First let me state that no one, and I mean no one, believes in the necessity of being a "hearer" of the word of God any more than I. This is one way faith is formed in the believer, *"So then faith cometh by hearing, and hearing by the word of God"* – (Rom. 10:17).

Let me also state that believing the word of God is imperative to the Christian life. Yet, just hearing and even believing the word of God "alone" cannot fully change you. It will bring light, it reveals the will and revelation of God, but that does not within itself transform the believer.

So many believe that if they just obey certain rules and obtain a certain amount of knowledge of the word, it will be sufficient. We often quote John 8:32, *"And ye shall know the truth, and the truth shall make you free."* Yet I've met a lot of people over the years who had great scriptural knowledge. They could quote chapters, were avid readers of the scriptures, they were extremely educated in biblical studies, yet having been around them for a while I knew they were "not free!" They had the knowledge of the truth, but were still battling the "Man In The Mirror" syndrome. I've known many others who obeyed all the laws of religion and then some, yet again they were not free.

Jesus preached and taught his twelve disciples for three and a half years. They lived in a perpetual School of Christ. From sun up till they lay down at night for sleep, He was teaching them the scriptures and deeper truths of the Kingdom of God. It is hard to even comprehend that after three and a half years, these twelve blessed disciples who lived and were taught in a Bible school like no other, on graduation day were still fumbling, doubting, undependable, and yes, sinning unspiritual reeds that you could not lean on in a time of crisis.

I am not taking up for ignorance, nor am I against biblical education. To have the first with the absence of the latter is usually a negative thing and often hurts the work of the Kingdom. Yet with all our getting of knowledge and learning over the last several decades, we have bypassed something of great importance in the church, and that is "an experience." The truth is not just words on a page, but a Person. I myself have cringed at the ignorance and misuse of the word of God by those who are mainly "experience oriented." Yet, when I say experience, I am not just talking about an emotional demonstration (and I am not against emotions nor demonstrative worship), but a life changing experience, which is the greatest supernatural phenomenon of all! An experience where we are changed! *"Who also hath made us able ministers of the new testament; not of the letter, but of the spirit: for the letter killeth, but the spirit giveth life"* – (2Cor. 3:6).

Life is a Person that we must experience, not just know about! That Person is Christ, *"And the Word was made flesh, and dwelt among us"* – (John 1:14).

Chapter 5

What Then Can Change Me?

WHAT is the answer to my struggle with the "Man In The Mirror" syndrome? What then can change me?

Although I had read the answer many times in scripture, somehow the "veil" had affected my "seeing." Although I knew, my knowing was dimmed somehow. The answer has always been there. There are two mirrors. Our problem has always been this.

We behold ourselves in the mirror of God's holy word. We see ourselves in this light, then we walk away and after a period of hours, days or weeks, we forget the man we saw in the mirror – his defects, blemishes, even sins. Later we are again brought before the mirror, the agonizing process is repeated and for most believers it becomes a never-ending cycle throughout their Christian life.

For the answer to, what can change me? We must find the *"SECOND MIRROR"*! There we can be changed and transformed into His likeness. In fact, this is the only place we can be delivered and freed from the "Man In The Mirror" syndrome!

Often in the Bible when the word "glass" is used it is describing what we today call a mirror. They were commonly made from polished plates of metal, such as brass. The metal being highly polished so the reflection of the person would be visible. The reflection would be visible, if there was nothing to dim the light, wherein again the "veil" comes to mind. Almost always when this word is used in the Bible in a spiritual connotation, it not meant for good. Such "veils" have hidden the deeper truth and revelation our hearts have searched and longed for. It has kept us on the "Merry-Go-Round" of coming before the first mirror, seeing ourselves, forgetting, and then repeating the process over and over.

I have already stated that hearing and even believing the word alone cannot change us. There has to be more than just the seeing and knowing of our defects, blemishes and sins. There must be "divine" encounters that bring a change and transformation in our lives.

In the thirty-fourth chapter of Exodus, Moses is in the mountain with God. The previous trips there were to receive the word of God, the Law, the Ten Commandments. No writer – even the most gifted – could ever pen the words to describe these experiences that Moses had with God, in giving him all the laws and commandments for the children of Israel to live by.

I want to again challenge our thinking here. After all these trips up into the mountain, hearing and receiving the word of God, it is obvious it had very little effect on the man Moses! Yes the word of God brings light, revelation, faith and it does sanctify, *"Sanctify them through thy truth: thy word is truth"* (John 17:17). Yet that alone did not seem to have the life and character changing effect on Moses that a later trip and experience up the same mountain had on him.

After he comes down from the holy mountain with the Ten Commandments in his hands, he draws near the camp of the children of Israel and hears the vulgarity, and then he witnesses the dancing around the golden calf and idolatry. This man of God whose name is mentioned in the Bible only second to Christ becomes so angry, he breaks the holy tablets of the Ten Commandments into thousands of pieces. Commandments written by the hand of God himself, *"And it came to pass at the end of forty days and forty nights, that the LORD gave me the two tables of stone, even the tables of the covenant" (Deut. 9:11),* are now lying scattered over the ground and rocks at the feet of Moses!

Those trips up the mountain to hear and receive the word, the law from God Himself, obviously didn't bring the needed change in this great man. I am convinced that this holy Prophet of God had what we call today an "anger management" problem! I know some will say, how can you diagnose Moses with such a fault thousands of years after he is dead? Let us go to another episode in his life. It happens by the brook Meribah.

"And the LORD spake unto Moses, saying, Take the rod, and gather thou the assembly together, thou, and Aaron thy brother, and speak ye unto the rock before their eyes; and it shall give forth his water, and thou shalt bring forth to them water out of the rock: so thou shalt give the congregation and their beasts drink. And Moses took the rod from before the LORD, as he commanded him. And Moses and Aaron gathered the congregation together before the rock, and he said unto them, Hear now, ye rebels; must we fetch you water out of this rock? And Moses lifted up his hand, and with his rod he smote the rock twice: and the water came out abundantly, and the congregation drank, and their beasts also. And the LORD spake unto Moses and Aaron" – (Num. 20:7-11).

In a fit of anger Moses disobeys the Lord's command to speak only to the rock. We've already seen his anger cause him to break the holy commandments written on stone by the hand of God! Some would say, this couldn't have been such a serious issue within Moses the great "Prophet" of God, and deliverer of His people. It was serious enough to keep him from going into the promise land! *"Because ye believed me not, to sanctify me in the eyes of the children of Israel, therefore ye shall not bring this congregation into the land which I have given them. This is the water of Meribah; because the children of Israel strove with the LORD, and he was sanctified in them"* – (Num. 20:12-13).

If this had been a matter of "righteous indignation," Moses would most likely not have been excluded from leading the Israelites across the Jordan. His moment of uncontrolled, unsanctified anger cost a heavy price.

How many of us in a moment of "flash" anger have said, done, or acted in some way that displeased the Lord? Even at times feeling justified because we believed we were "right." I remember, a few times over the years that in a moment of "instant" anger or "seething" anger that slowly built up inside, I've had to apologize to my wife, other believers and even someone in an airport that I didn't even know. At first you feel justified, then you quickly realize Jesus would not have reacted that way. While I asked forgiveness of God and those I demonstrated my anger too, I fully understood that I wasn't as much like Christ as I thought and certainly desired to be. I was experiencing the *"Man In The Mirror"* syndrome. It never brings me comfort to know that I am not alone. I want to be like Him, no excuses.

While the word of the Lord alone did not change Moses, an experience on a subsequent trip to the mountain where God's presence was abiding, did impact him dramatically. After Moses received the Law, the word of God, He then manifested a level of fleshly anger that cost him his right to lead Israel into the promise land. Following this, Moses cries out one day from deep in his heart, *"And he said, I beseech Thee, shew me Thy glory"* – (Ex. 33:18).

This was not a cry for God to show him more "glory manifestations," fire, smoke and light, but for Jehovah to reveal to him His character, His holiness, His ways. I have no doubt this is the request God had been waiting for from the man Moses. Here is the Lord's reply, *"And he said, I will make all My goodness pass before thee, and I will proclaim the name of the LORD before thee; and will be gracious to whom I will be gracious, and will shew mercy on whom I will shew mercy. And he said, Thou canst not see My face: for there shall no man see Me, and live. And the LORD said, Behold, there is a place by*

Me, and thou shalt stand upon a rock: And it shall come to pass, while My glory passeth by, that I will put thee in a clift of the rock, and will cover thee with My hand while I pass by: And I will take away Mine hand, and thou shalt see My back parts: but My face shall not be seen" – (Ex. 33:19-23).

This revelation of God's glory, His character, His ways, and His holiness wrought a "life altering" and "visible" change in Moses beyond anything he had experienced before. Nothing had ever happened on the mountain with God that had so revolutionized his life as the beholding of His "character," "nature," His ways and "seeing His back parts." After his experience of seeing "God's Glory," Moses comes down off the mountain with that very glory emanating out of the pigment in his face. *"And when Aaron and all the children of Israel saw Moses, behold, the skin of his face shone; and they were afraid to come nigh him"* (Ex. 34:30). The word "shone" in the Hebrew means, to "push out like horns," like "rays of light." This was the appearance of Moses after "seeing His glory." Because it frightened the people it says in verse 35, that Moses put the veil upon his face, until he went in to speak with God in the tabernacle.

This asking of Moses to veil his face was a costly mistake for the people. If they had only stared into this glory long enough, it could have changed them. But the veil kept them from "seeing." *"And not as Moses, which put a veil over his face, that the children of Israel could not steadfastly look to the end of that which is abolished"* – (2Cor. 3:13).

This was shadow and type. Though this veil literally blocked the rays of glory coming from Moses face, the great truth here is that it kept them from seeing the fulfillment of the law through Jesus Christ! *"Nevertheless when it shall turn to the lord, the veil shall be taken away. Now the lord is that spirit: and where the spirit of the lord is, there is liberty."* – (2Cor. 3:16).

They would have beheld the glory of the Old Testament Christ. Through Whom all the law was fulfilled. This according not only to the Apostle Paul in the New Testament but also foretold by Isaiah *"And he will destroy in this mountain the face of the covering cast over all people, and the veil that is spread over all nations"* – (Isa. 25:7).

Just Whom did Moses see? Who was the "Rock" that the Apostle Paul declared followed them through the desert? When he wrote in 1Corinthians 10:4 *"And did all drink the same spiritual drink: for they drank of that spiritual Rock that followed them: and that Rock was Christ."*

Who was the "Captain of the 'Lord's host'" that Joshua later saw in Joshua 5:14-15, when preparing to take the land? If it was the "Glory" of the one upon Moses face that was to fulfill the law, then it is obvious. *"Think not that I am come to destroy the law, or the prophets: I am not come to destroy, but to fulfill"* (Matt. 5:17). The Apostle John declared that, Isaiah saw the "Glory" of the Old Testament Christ in the sixth chapter of Isaiah. When Isaiah saw him "high and lifted up." *"These things said Esaias, when he saw His glory, and spake of Him"* – (John 12:41).

It is without doubt that the children of Israel were looking into the "Glory" of the one who would come and "fulfill all righteousness." The One, who would come and become the "eternal sacrifice." The One who Isaiah, David, Zechariah and many others in the Old Testament prophesied of, that was to come and be the Messiah and Savior of the world. Sadly, they did not want to behold His glory in the face of Moses, just as many who call themselves Christians today, refuse to "look into" and "behold" His glory, so that they can be changed and free from the "Man In The Mirror" syndrome. Some now ask after all this, "What is the answer to the 'Man In The Mirror' syndrome? What can make me and form me into the image of Christ? Into the man or woman who manifests the character of Christ, thinks like Christ, demonstrates and manifests Christ?" We must remember, it's not just in hearing or knowing truth, not just in obeying rules alone, not just in keeping laws.

That alone is what is known as religion.

Chapter 6

The Second Mirror

THE stone tablets of the Ten Commandments were the mirror of the law and when the people saw it, they measured their lives by it. Like as beholding themselves in a mirror. They had to offer sacrifices to atone for their failures and sins. Year by year, the blood from the sacrificial animals ran like a river, thus the "Merry-Go-Round."

Some years ago my mentor and I were in Denver, Colorado and I was the morning speaker in the meeting we were preaching together. I remember before my prepared sermon began, I shared how the Lord was dealing with me about James 1:22-24. I was sharing with the congregation about the "Merry-Go-Round" and how I know there is surely an answer to such struggles with the "old man." Of course, the answer was there in the scriptures all along. It is always there, yet again the "veil" often shadows it. Can I explain these things? No. But I have found that this is God's way with us, here a little, there a little, line upon line, precept upon precept.

Then in His own time in -- a spiritual sense – the following verse was "highlighted" in my spirit, and my understanding began to grow concerning the answer. I have no other way to explain than this. It is something that I had a knowledge of, yet it wasn't "magnified" in me. One day, the Lord took me to the verse, *"But we all, with open face beholding as in a glass the glory of the lord, are changed into the same image from glory to glory even as by the Spirit of the lord"* – (2Cor. 3:18).

The Children of Israel could not see beyond the veil that covered Moses' glory covered face, but now it has been removed for those who want to see past the "ministration of condemnation." *"For if the ministration of condemnation be glory, much more doth the ministration of righteousness exceed in glory"* – (2Cor. 3:9).

Who are we looking at in the glass? Jesus, the Christ, the very Son of God; His image, His glory, His likeness, and if we, behold Him continually, daily coming into His presence in the mirror of His glory, we shall be changed. The word "changed" in the Greek is *met-am-or-fo'-o*: to transform, literally or figuratively metamorphose, to transfigure. We use the word "metamorphosis" which means to "become transformed." Webster's dictionary states that it is a change that comes especially supernaturally. It is a process of change, remember the scriptures declare from "glory to glory."

I've often used this illustration when preaching concerning this:

"As child we would go up to an adult with a cocoon in our hand and ask, 'What is this?' We would be told, 'That has a beautiful butterfly inside of it, so put it back where you found it. Don't open it, and one day the butterfly inside will come out.' They never said it had to go through a *metamorphosis,* a change, a process of transforming over time. It is unlikely that even with such information it wouldn't have mattered to a mischievous child, so the cocoon was opened anyway to appease our curious little minds. And guess what? The child is shocked that the adults had not told all the facts, because, inside wasn't a beautiful butterfly, but an ugly, wormy looking insect. We children didn't understand *metamorphosis.* If we had just left the cocoon alone for a season of time, the wormy little insect would have transformed into a beautiful butterfly."

As Christians we find that in spite of our sanctification, we sometimes have issues. We battle things of the flesh and not always so perfectly. If we will daily go before and into His presence, we will go through a spiritual and supernatural "metamorphosis," and will be changed into His image, His character and take on His likeness and holiness. Does the word of God give us a scriptural basis for this? Absolutely, *"And be not conformed to this world: but be ye transformed {metamorphose} by the renewing of your mind, that ye may prove what is that good, and acceptable, and perfect, will of God"* – (Rom..12:2).

"My little children, of whom I travail in birth again until Christ be formed {fashioned} in you – (Gal. 4:19).

"Till we all come in the unity of the faith, and of the knowledge {gr: full discernment} of the Son of God unto a perfect man, unto the measure of the stature of the fullness of Christ – (Eph. 4:13).

It is troubling to note that many today simply make excuses and seem to be have a "light" and "trivial" attitude about dealing with the sins and failures of believers. Without doubt a message that constantly condemns, rarely, if ever brings change to failing Christians. On the other side, we should be honest and state that there is a problem, there are issues, yet there is hope. There is a promise of victory and of overcoming power made to the believer who will be honest with God and separate themselves to go into His presence consistently. Not just when one can find the time, or periodically and with a "quick in and out" effort. This is the most important thing a believer in Christ can do, to seek the holy face of God, to spend time in the presence of Jesus, daily. God has given us His word: If we will, then He will, and the change will come!

How can we ever be like Jesus? How can we be perfect, and formed in His image, His character, and His holiness, seeing that we fail Him so much, and we often struggle to do His will and keep His commandments. You can struggle and try in your flesh. You can beat yourself up over and over, repent of failing to be like Christ, but you cannot do it in your own ability. Your own works and self-effort can never make it happen.

"How can this thing be?", Mary asked such a question of the angel, after his announcement to her, saying she was chosen to be the one who would give birth to the Messiah. She couldn't comprehend such a thing happening to her. His reply, *"And the angel answered and said unto her, The Holy Ghost shall come upon thee, and the power of the Highest shall overshadow thee"* – (Luke 1:35).

There is no other way to be free from the "Man In The Mirror" syndrome than by the power of the Holy Spirit, conforming us into the image of Christ! Some would say, but I am holy, I am godly, I am a Christian, I know my life is pleasing to God! Really?

A friend some years ago who, was an associate in his father's church told me this story. He said, he started a teaching series on Wednesday nights, based on the "words of Christ in red." After a couple of lessons, he said he was shocked at how the people became angry at what he was teaching. This was a fundamental Pentecostal church. I didn't want to doubt him, but I struggled with how, this was possible, the words of Christ in red? Every believer should love these precious words as they do all scripture. So I took some time and read through again the New Testament covering the words of Jesus. It didn't take long for me to understand what happened.

Most Christians love to proclaim how much we love Jesus and of our desire to keep His commandments. The proclaiming part is quite easy; it's the actual doing that's difficult. Jesus gave what I call the "acid test" of what constitutes a "true" follower and a "real" disciple. In the sixth chapter of Luke He was telling those around Him what they must do as believers. He said, "If someone took your cloke, let them have your coat also." To put that in a modern perspective, I'll share an experience I had some years ago: Someone stole my pressure washer. It cost a few hundred dollars and was something I considered needful. I was angry and wanted to find out for sure who the person was that stole it. My purpose for finding out the particular thief was not to give them the soap and the fuel to go along with it, but to have them arrested! Yes, I was that aggravated about having it taken from my property. Yet Jesus said, give them what goes along with it, and I was convicted by my attitude and feelings of anger. As you read this, don't feel so sanctimonious. Jesus also declared that we were to "love our neighbor as ourselves," and let's be honest, if your neighbor erected his fence up a foot over and across your property line, would you have the property re-surveyed and give him that extra foot of property he had taken? If your cute little dog that you cherish so much crossed over once to many times into your neighbor's yard and he shot it with say, a pellet gun, would you still love and be kind to them? Jesus said, "If someone smites us on our cheek, that we are to turn and offer him or her the other." Let's be honest, how many really would allow someone to slap you in the face without some angry retaliation? Yet, Jesus said, to not slap back.

It is very easy to testify to how much we love Jesus and all those around us, and how we desire to keep His commandments, but actually doing it is not as easy as we imagine. That's why we need to be changed into His likeness and go through a metamorphosis of His character and nature.

Again, this is why I constantly preach and write about being filled with the Holy Spirit. He alone can bring this supernatural change in us. The old commentators give such a grand and wonderful picture of this supernatural phenomenon. Adam Clarke stated concerning 2Corinthians 3:18, *"'As by the Spirit of the Lord,'* by the energy of that Spirit of Christ which gives life and being to all the promises of the gospel; and thus we are made partakers of the divine nature and escape all the corruptions that are in the world. Now as mirrors among the Jews, Greeks, and Romans, were made of highly polished metal, it would often happen, especially in strong light, that the face would be greatly illuminated by this strongly reflected light and to this circumstance the apostle seems here to allude. So by earnestly contemplating the gospel of Jesus, and believing on him who is its Author, the soul becomes illuminated with His divine splendor for this sacred mirror reflects back on the believing soul the image of Him whose perfections it exhibits; and thus we see the glorious form after which our minds are to be fashioned; and by believing and receiving the influence of His Spirit, our form is changed into the same image, which we behold there."

Albert Barnes wrote, "*'As by the Spirit of the Lord,'* it is done by the Holy Spirit, procured or imparted by the Lord Jesus. This sentiment is in accordance with that which prevails everywhere in the bible that is by the Holy Spirit alone that the heart is changed and purified. And the object of the statement here is, doubtless, to prevent the supposition that the change from 'glory to glory' was produced in any sense by the mere contemplation of the truth, it was by the Spirit of God alone that the heart was changed.'"

Barnes continued: "So it is in regard to the opinions and feelings which from any cause we are in the habit of bringing before our minds. It is the way by which people become corrupted in their sentiments and feelings, in their contact with the world; it is the way in which amusements, and the company of the frivolous and the dissipated possess so much power; it the way in which the young and inexperienced are beguiled and ruined; and it is the way in which Christians dim the luster of their piety, and obscure the brightness of their religion by their contact with the happy and fashionable world. It is on the same great principle that Paul says that by contemplating the glory of God in the gospel, we become insensibly but certainly conformed to the same image and made like the redeemer. His image will be reflected on us. We shall imbibe his sentiments, catch his feelings, and be molded into the image of his own purity such is the great and wise law of our nature; and it is on this principle and by this means that God designs we should be made pure on earth, and kept pure in heaven forever."

Finally, the great Prophet Isaiah's own experience gives us

insight to how coming into Christ's presence, and daily into His glory can change and make us available for the Lord to use us:

"In the year that king Uzziah died I saw also the Lord sitting upon a throne, high and lifted up, and His train filled the temple. Above it stood the seraphims: each one had six wings; with twain he covered his face, and with twain he covered his feet, and with twain he did fly. And one cried unto another, and said, Holy, holy, holy, is the LORD of hosts: the whole earth is full of His glory. And the posts of the door moved at the voice of him that cried, and the house was filled with smoke. Then said I, Woe is me! for I am undone; because I am a man of unclean lips, and I dwell in the midst of a people of unclean lips: for mine eyes have seen the King, the LORD of hosts. Then flew one of the seraphims unto me, having a live coal in his hand, which he had taken with the tongs from off the altar: And he laid it upon my mouth, and said, Lo, this hath touched thy lips; and thine iniquity is taken away, and thy sin purged. Also I heard the voice of the Lord, saying, Whom shall I send, and who will go for us? Then said I, Here am I; send me." – (Isa. 6:1).

First Isaiah saw and beheld the glory of the Old Testament Christ as declared in John 12:41 – "These things said Esaias, when he saw His glory, and spake of Him." Remember, in His presence, His glory, we are changed. Did the great prophet Isaiah need to be changed? Was he experiencing some "Man In The Mirror" issues? Obviously, and he declared as much when he said, *"Woe is me! for I am undone; because I am a man of unclean lips."* This kind of "inward" revelation concerning one of the greatest Old Testament prophets could only be revealed in the presence of Christ, beholding His glory. Was there a "metamorphosis" of change? Of course, and we see this in verses six and seven, when the angel takes tongs from the altar with a live coal and touches the prophet's lips; his sin now purged, a work of sanctification is wrought. Now Isaiah is ready for the Lord's work and prepared to fulfill His will. He hears the voice of the Lord, *"Whom shall I send, and who will go for us?"*

Isaiah cries out, *"Here am I: send me."*

Is this your heart's cry? Lord, I want to be used by you! I want to be sent forth as a holy vessel. I am weary of the continuous battle with the "Man In The Mirror" and my desire is to come daily into your presence and be changed from "glory to glory."

From this day forth, be determined to enter in to that place we come to meet with Him and linger in His presence and holiness. Let us do this on a consistent daily basis, until we are changed; until we go through a "metamorphosis" of His likeness. This is where we will die daily to self and are transformed into His likeness. How can this thing be? Only through and by the Holy Spirit, Who alone can change us into His image.

Will we be sanctified? Yes, a thousand times yes; and in the biblical teaching of sanctification. The Bible declares in 1Corinthians 1:30, *"But of Him are ye in Christ Jesus, who of God is made unto us wisdom, and righteousness, and sanctification, and redemption."*

There is an old song that sums it all up –

> "Turn your eyes upon Jesus,
> look full into His wonderful face,
> and the things of earth will grow strangely dim,
> in the light of His marvelous grace."

www.ingramcontent.com/pod-product-compliance
Lightning Source LLC
Chambersburg PA
CBHW061313040426
42444CB00010B/2623